Dec's Super Specs

by Katie Dale

illustrated by Berta Maluenda

OXFORD
UNIVERSITY PRESS

Dec found it difficult to talk to people. He found it tricky to make friends, too.

Dec loved football, but he was too shy to join in.

Dec struggled to see the teacher's writing.

"Can anyone work out this fraction?" the teacher asked.

Dec solved the maths problem in his head.
He didn't want to raise his hand.

Dec's mum took him to get his sight tested.

Dec peered at the little letters. They were so difficult to read.

"You need glasses," Mum said. "Let's choose some nice ones."

"I don't want to wear glasses!" Dec protested. "They'll look funny!"

“They won’t!” Dec’s mum said. “Look, there’s a huge selection of lovely frames. Try some on and see.”

Dec put on round specs, then square ones. Then he tried some cool glasses with a jazzy design.

“Excuse me, sir,” Dec’s mum said to Dec. “Have you seen my son?”

“Mum, it’s me!” Dec cried.

“Dec?” Mum gasped. “I didn’t recognise you in those lovely specs!”

“Didn’t you?” Dec glanced at his reflection.

He looked really different with glasses on! Just like Superman! He was Super-Dec!

Dec climbed the hill to school the next day. He felt amazing with his new glasses on. He could see clearly for the first time!

Dec spotted Reece, a boy from his class. Instead of being timid, Dec waved.

"Hi!" Reece called. "Nice specs!"

"Thanks!" Dec said, beaming. "Let's walk to school together!"

Suddenly, Dec didn't feel shy, and he even cracked a joke.

"What did one hat say to the other?
You wait here, I'll go on *a head*!" Dec said.

Reece giggled and Dec began to feel like Super-Dec!

Dec could see everything the teacher wrote and drew without squinting!

"What animal is this?" the teacher asked.

Dec raised his hand confidently.

"It's a tortoise," Dec said. "Tortoises can live for over one hundred years. A group of tortoises is known as a 'creep'."

"Yes! Exactly right!" the teacher said.

Dec smiled.

At lunch, Dec joined in playing football. He kicked the ball into the net and everyone cheered. Dec loved being Super-Dec!

Then Alice patted Dec's back and his specs fell off! Dec felt himself freeze. His confidence vanished and his pulse raced. Without his glasses, everyone would recognise him!

However, to Dec's surprise, Reece picked up the specs.

"Here you go, Dec!" Reece said, giving them back to him. "You might need these, buddy!"

Dec was shocked. “You knew it was me all along?”

“I know you! I wave at you every morning,” Reece grinned.

“Do you?” Dec gasped. “I never saw you!”

"I've wanted to be your friend for ages," Reece said. "I'm so glad you finally stopped hiding in your shell, like a tortoise!"

"Me, too," Dec giggled.

“Come and play, Dec!” his new friends cried.

Dec beamed. Glasses or no glasses, he felt totally super!

Retell the Story

Encourage students to use the pictures to retell the story.